The Second St. Poems

Bilingual Press/Editorial Bilingüe

General Editor
Gary D. Keller

Managing Editor
Karen S. Van Hooft

Senior Editor
Mary M. Keller

Editorial Board
Juan Goytisolo
Francisco Jiménez
Eduardo Rivera
Severo Sarduy
Mario Vargas Llosa

Address
Bilingual Press
Department of Foreign Languages
and Bilingual Studies
217 New Alexander
EASTERN MICHIGAN UNIVERSITY
Ypsilanti, Michigan 48197
313-487-0042

The
Second St. Poems

Beverly Silva

Bilingual Press/Editorial Bilingüe
YPSILANTI, MICHIGAN

ISBN: 0-916950-39-5

Library of Congress Catalog Card Number: 83-70276

PRINTED IN THE UNITED STATES OF AMERICA

Cover design by Larry Scheffler

Acknowledgments

*Grateful appreciation is expressed to the following individuals and pub-
lications for permission to reprint previously published or accepted poems
that appear in this volume:*

Beulah Linnell, chairman of authors committee, for "Second St.," *California in
Rhyme and Rhythm, I* (Hayward, CA: California Historical Society, 1980), p. 68.
Ronald Grossman, editor, for "Hey You!," *Broken Streets* (Bristol, CT), Vol. III
(1981), p. 9.
James MaHood, editor, for "Two Brothers," scheduled to appear in his anthology
Erotic Love Poems.
Maurice Kenny, co-editor, for "Wetbacks," scheduled to appear in *Contact II.*

CONTENTS

Introduction

A SPACE OF HER OWN:
THE SECOND ST. POEMS
BY BEVERLY SILVA

María Inés Lagos-Pope

The Second St. Poems by Beverly Silva constitute a search, a woman's search for her own path and her own self. In her quest for definition, the poetic I watches, discovers, moves, finding pleasure and joy in personal relationships, everyday occurrences, and daily chores. Although the mood may be nostalgic or even painful at times, the feeling of being part of a world, of sharing a place and a tradition with others, is a constant source of strength and energy. Deeply rooted in Chicano culture and space, these poems go beyond the local to encompass the experience of being a contemporary woman.

Silva's poetry is a profoundly personal introspective poetry that reflects the experience of being a Chicana today in California. The poems in this collection refer to a very distinct and concrete period in Silva's life, the years when she lived in downtown San José trying to make a living and survive alone after finishing her university studies. During these transitional years she must find her way as an independent woman, one who has already raised her children and is now starting a new life. Since these poems are strongly tied to her life experience, and given the fact that this is her first collection of poems to be published as a book, it seems pertinent to refer briefly to her biography.[1]

Beverly Silva was born in Los Angeles in the 1930s. She spent her childhood years in many different places, living with her Mexican grandparents after her parents' divorce and later with her mother when she remarried. Her grandfather was a master story-teller, and Silva developed a taste for literature and languages at an early age. She wanted to be a writer and go to college, but her parents put her in a vocational-secretarial course and did not allow her to pursue the education she desired.

9

Silva married three times and had four children. Her first husband, a logger, died in an accident after five weeks of marriage. She had been married for almost six years to her second husband, with whom she shared a love of poetry, music and writing, when he suffered a mental breakdown and was confined to a state hospital. Upon his release from the hospital he ran off and she never saw him again. Her third marriage, to an older man, lasted thirteen years. During this period she met, for the first time in her life, educated people who had read the books she had enjoyed in solitude.

When her youngest child entered school in 1969, she registered at San José City College. Although she did not participate actively in the student movement of the late sixties and early seventies as she would have liked, the atmosphere of the period had a strong impact on her life. She confesses that she "was so emotionally changed by these events that I was never able to go back to old ways of living." She left her husband and the security he represented and went to live in downtown San José with her three daughters. She had to earn a living, for which she was not at all prepared, and continued going to school. She graduated with an M.A. in English from San José State University in 1976. She was unemployed for some time and went through the same difficulties she had experienced as a student, but by this time she had learned to face her problems "head on," she says. In 1980 she began teaching English as a second language and has since moved to East San José. In the summer of 1981 she went to Mexico for the first time. Throughout this period she has pursued her interest in writing, and her work has been increasingly recognized.

There are at least two traditions to which it is necessary to refer in order to establish a frame of reference for discussing Silva's work. First, her poetry is inscribed in the Chicano tradition, and secondly it has ties with the American feminist movement. Both trends, which have many features in common with regard to their political goals and the artistic developments that they have inspired, had as one point of departure the student movement of the late sixties and early seventies, which had a decisive impact on Silva's work. The two movements attempt to assert an identity, argue against the belief that patriarchal discourse is universal, and propose that new types of discourse must be developed in order to adequately express the experiences of minority and marginal groups and thus create a space of their own in both literature and society.[2] Nevertheless, although the goals of these groups are similar, their struggle had different origins, and their members have suffered from different types of oppression. For this reason it is necessary to establish a distinction between them.

The relationship between personal experience and literary creation has been one of the topics that critics of Chicano literature and feminist literary critics have confronted rather than avoided. Recent Chicano and feminist works have served as vehicles of expression for Chicanos and women to articulate realities that had been absent from literature and to deal with themes that had been considered unworthy of artistic endeavor by patriarchal discourse or viewed as deviant by male critics and writers. Thus, for Chicanos and women, literature has contributed to the development of a sense of identity and self-discovery, and at the same time that it has served as a means of attaining self-knowledge it has chronicled their struggle. Since for the first time in the history of literature these realities have found, as a concerted movement, access to and recognition in society, it has been necessary to describe and record personal experiences that have stressed the strong links between the cultural, the social and the personal.

Before proceeding to the analysis of Silva's collection I will examine the Chicano tradition from which her poems emerge and the literary strategies that recent American and Latin American women poets have developed in order to create a means of expression to adequately expose the female consciousness.

During the past decade, critics of Chicano literature have concentrated on a number of critical and cultural issues in order to establish a theoretical framework and develop appropriate approaches for the analysis of recent Chicano literary works. Among the topics that have been debated are the origins of Chicano culture and its literature; the criteria to be applied in order to identify Chicano literature, since there are texts written in Spanish, in English, or in both languages; whether Chicano literature should be classified as Latin American "American" literature; and the methodology most suitable to its analysis.

Before proceeding further with this discussion it seems appropriate to clarify what is understood by the term Chicano.

Although this is a complex question that has given rise to serious debates, it is helpful and illuminating for our purposes to remember Octavio Paz's answer when he was asked about the difference between Mexicans and Chicanos:

> Los orígenes son los mismos, pero hemos vivido en ambientes diferentes y con unas evoluciones diferentes. Esto es lo que nos caracteriza: comunidad de origen, comunidad cultural y al mismo tiempo diferencias sociales, culturales y económicas... que son consecuencia de la historia diferente del grupo chicano y del mexicano.[3]

The term Mexican-American, on the other hand, points toward the origins and affiliation of the present Chicano population. Juan Bruce-Novoa has aptly observed that Chicanos are neither Mexican nor American but:

> the space (not the hyphen) between the two, the intercultural nothing of that space, pushing the two out and apart as we build our own separate reality, while at the same time creating strong bonds of interlocking tension that hold the two in relationship. Each Chicano writer opens a space for its own existence and adds to the total space of Chicano art as well as Art itself.[4]

The distinction made by Bruce-Novoa is especially useful in approaching Silva's work, since with her collection of poems she is creating her own space not only as a Chicano, by expanding Chicano art and expression, but also as a woman, as a Chicana poet. The experience of being in-between, of being at a crossroads, and the task of finding a place in society are fundamental concerns not only for Chicanos but for women as well. The poetic I in *The Second St. Poems* is between East and West San José, between ordinary life in the barrio and the life of an intellectual at the university, between motherhood and career, between her Mexican values and heritage and her life in the United States. As we have seen from her biographical data, Silva is not only searching for a space in Chicano literature but also in life.

Many critics have underscored the relevance of the oral tradition to recent Chicano literature. Arturo Madrid in his article "La problemática de la experiencia y la literatura chicana" suggests that the geographic isolation of the old Mexican territories that today constitute the American Southwest was one of the crucial factors in the historical and cultural development of the region in the nineteenth century.[5] Although Spanish was cultivated by an elite, the language of commerce and business transactions was English. However, the Mexican masses did not receive instruction in either of the two languages and in this way they remained deprived of access to the written word. Madrid asserts that one of the direct sources of Chicano literature as developed in the last fifteen years is the old oral tradition in the form of *baladas, cuentos, décimas, romances,* and especially the *corrido,* which already contained the seed of what became the Chicano literature of protest:

> [el corrido] abarcaba toda la problemática del mexicano en los Estados Unidos: los abusos de los gringos, las agresiones de los rinches, el heroísmo de los valientes, la maestría de los vaqueros, los sufrimientos de los braceros, las humillaciones de los refugiados, las desgracias de los renegados, las tragedias de los repatriados, las quejas de los recién llegados, las protestas de los mexicano-norteamericanos.[6]

After a first stage characterized by aggressive struggle and protest in order to establish themselves and keep their identity among the American plurality and diversity, Chicano writers have reached, according to Salvador Rodríguez del Pino, the stage of "invención." He maintains that with "el alejamiento de modelos imitativos, los escritores y poetas están ahora creando e inventando una literatura que parte de lo chicano pero que incluye la calidad de lo humano universal."[7] But, although the relationship between social and political tension and poetry that distinguished contemporary Chicano literature in its beginnings has diminished, and although it has been replaced by more personal and intimate creations, the new poetry still reflects "the private experiences of the poet in time and space,"[8] thus continuing to be, primarily, a referential poetry.

Most critics have emphasized that Chicano literature, through its combative character, has served the cause of the Chicano people by helping reassert its tradition and establish its identity. They also agree that although Chicano literature has its origins in Mexican literature and tradition, it constitutes a very distinct and different entity. Many of them concur that in the future it will most probably be a literature written almost entirely in English, since that is the language of the new generations who have had access to a college education. In Silva's case, the poet uses English as her primary language in all the poems in the present collection except one, "Sin Ti Yo No Soy Nada," which as its title suggests is a love poem. When the speaker switches to Spanish it is to express closeness, warm feelings, to recall the Mexican tradition, or to communicate her own values or other special effects.[9]

It is fitting then to ask ourselves whether this literature written in the United States should be considered part of United States literature or Latin American literature. In approaching this complex question one has to take into account not only the cultural heritage to which it belongs but the language in which it is written as well. There is Chicano literature being written exclusively in Spanish or in English and Chicano literature that uses different degrees of bilingualism or code-switching. Critics are divided on this matter. Some, including Santiago Daydí-Tolson, consider it a Latin American literature; others, among them Rolando Hinojosa, are inclined to regard it as a United States literature.[10] In my view, since literature as a form of language is communication, the language question is crucial. If the work is written in English it is clearly out of reach for the Spanish-speaking public of Latin America. However, if it is bilingual or written in Spanish it raises other questions.

The experience these writers convey is that of people of Mexican descent who have lived in the United States sometimes for generations; in other words, it is that of a minority culture that has confronted realities quite different from those that Latin Americans living in their own countries have had to face. For these reasons I agree with Rolando Hinojosa when he states that Chicano literature "is a United States literature and it is, at times, monolingual, [at times] bilingual."[11] Moreover, with respect to the problem of language Hinojosa suggests that "the languages will most probably coexist for some time, but, and this is a personal observation, I fear that Spanish will lose out in the long run. English, most certainly, will win in the non-fiction areas of literature."[12] The critic warns, however, about being too categorical when dealing with so many complexities and possible combinations. But regardless of one's stance in this matter, what is important to acknowledge is that we are in the presence of a literature that is finding its modes of expression and asserting a tradition, and ultimately it will be judged by what its creative achievements may be.

Although in the past fifteen years Chicano literature has conquered a secure place in academic circles as well as in the publishing world, the Chicana is still striving for recognition and acceptance. In a 1977 interview Rolando Hinojosa was asked to name the works that in his judgment were the milestones of Chicano literature, and the author did not include any work by a woman.[13] However, in his overview of Chicano poetry Salvador Rodríguez del Pino devotes a few paragraphs to the work of Chicana poets. In this critic's opinion, due to the double oppression the Chicana has suffered for being Chicana and female, two poetic themes have stood out in her poetry: "la opresión del sistema y la temática de la opresión de la tradición machista chicana, herencia de la cultura mexicana."[14]

In 1969 Enriqueta Longanez y Vásquez, Chicana writer and activist, exhorted her Raza sisters to collaborate in the Chicano movement with the purpose of liberating both men and women. Longanez concluded her argument by saying:

> we must strive for the fulfillment of all as equals with the full capability and right to develop as humans. When the man can look upon "his" woman as HUMAN and with the love of BROTHERHOOD and EQUALITY, then and only then, can he feel the true meaning of liberation and equality himself. When we talk of equality in the Mexican-American movement we better be talking about TOTAL equality, beginning right where it all starts, AT HOME.[15]

But, because of the Hispanic tradition of women's submissiveness and macho pride, these goals were not easy to achieve for the Chicana inside the movement. While the struggle for Chicano rights was the main concern of La Raza and the idealization of its origins and exploration of its Mexican roots, the principal ideological direction, the needs of the Chicana not only had no priority but were considered to go against what Chicano culture stood for. Thus, the Chicana's claim for equality was seen as a desire to be like white women, "gringas" or "gabachas" as they are derogatorily called; in other words, it was viewed as indicative of the acculturation of the Mexican-American woman. Sylvia A. Gonzales refers to this dilemma in her article "La Chicana: Guadalupe or Malinche."

After analyzing the tradition that regards women as either virgins or prostitutes, she concludes with the optimistic assertion that it is indeed possible to eliminate sexism in Chicano culture and at the same time preserve the family and Chicano identity:

> Chicanos argue that Chicana feminism will lead to the destruction of the family and, thus, Chicano culture. This need not be so. As a matter of fact, Chicana feminism may well provide the vehicle for serious scholarship, cultural analysis, and group self-criticism. If Chicano males can free themselves of the phantasms of the past and their sexist causes and effects, will and intelligence can guide their lives instead and Chicano people will survive.[16]

Guadalupe Valdés, on the other hand, has a much more radical stance with respect to the role of women in Chicano culture. In her view, "the Mexican woman has been taught to take pride in her submissiveness, to want to be 'just a woman,' a baby machine, a cook and laundress, and possibly even a 'sainted mother' to an adoring male child... she has no dignity, no rights, and no voice." Valdés concludes by proposing that "if a tradition cannot offer freedom it must be discarded or destroyed."[17]

The Chicana certainly finds heself trapped in a dilemma that is difficult to resolve in a harmonious way. She belongs to a tradition that has kept woman in the role of wife and mother and at the same time she lives in a society that stresses the individual and that is going through a process of reassessing the role of women and their place in society. Valdés' attitude represents the new educated Chicana who does not want to accept an inferior or subservient condition just to perpetuate a tradition that has subjugated woman to man's will.

Even if the Chicana shares with Mexican and Latin American women the same traditions and family values, because of her intercultural heritage—Mexican and American—and because she participates in United States culture and is affected by the social and economic realities of this country, the Chicana's situation differs from that of her Latin American sisters. On the one hand, just as is the case with Latin American and other Third World women, the Chicana's plight is inseparable from that of her group. "As Chicanas we have found that we do not feel completely comfortable in the Women's Liberation Movement. We are not only concerned with ourselves but with the rest of La Raza. We want to work with our men in improving the social and economic conditions for our people," states Noemí Lorenzana.[18] On this point the Chicana is closer to Latin American women, who have repeated again and again that they do not conceive of a women's movement that does not attempt to liberate society as a whole rather than just focusing on the rights and condition of women.

An example of this attitude can be found in the positions taken by Latin American and other Third World women during the United Nations Conference on Women held in Mexico City in 1975. By rejecting the strategies of North American feminists, Third World representatives showed solidarity with the struggle of their peoples against economic and political oppression and demonstrated their view of American women as an integral part of American imperialism. This position has been strongly influenced by the colonial status of most Third World countries and by the authoritarian governments in power in many of the representatives' home countries in Latin America, factors which have made it impossible for these women to separate their needs from those of society at large. This trend can also be observed in their literature.[19] There is a strong tendency on the part of Latin American women writers to view the two struggles as flip sides of the same coin. Two notable contemporary examples are those of Rosario Ferré from Puerto Rico and the Uruguayan Cristina Peri Rossi. In the short stories and poems of *Papeles de Pandora* (1976), Ferré shows women's assertiveness through the rebelliousness of the female characters and their aggressive voices, and she relates their struggle to the political situation in her country. She suggests that there is a parallel between the colonial status of Puerto Rico and women's condition in society.[20]

In contrast, by living in the United States the Chicana participates, directly or indirectly, in the changes that have taken place in American society in the last decades with regard to the rights of women and minorities, who are gaining access to education and other spheres that had been closed to them before. The modern Chicana is far from being submissive and dependent or a homemaker content with the traditional roles of wife and mother like her ancestors.[21] I share Isabelle Navar's view that "the Chicana... is definitely a woman of the United States... strong, although faced

17

with many problems, emerging in her own identity with care and pride and vision."[22]

In many ways, then, the Chicana is closer in her struggle for freedom and liberation to American than to Mexican or Latin American women.[23] Some of the issues and themes Beverly Silva explores in her poetry reflect the condition of contemporary American women. The Mexican or the Latin American woman has not attained the sexual freedom or the economic independence of her American counterpart, the Chicana in this case, nor does she enjoy the options available to the latter. Silva's poems show a new direction in the Chicana's experience: throughout this collection the speaker suggests that even though she recognizes her roots to be in Mexico and in the barrio, she is not trapped by tradition; on the contrary, she values tradition, but on her own terms.

Although there is to a certain extent a tradition of poetry writing by women in Latin America that has defied the male order by expressing women's experience and female eroticism,[24] it has been the contemporary American women poets who have undauntedly broken away from the imposition of patriarchal values on women's lives and have spoken more openly about women's condition.

Noteworthy among the Latin Americans is the 17th-century Mexican nun Sor Juana Inés de la Cruz, who defended her freedom to write and study in the famous response to the Bishop of Puebla's condemnation of her intellectual activities. In her well-known poem "Hombres necios" she accuses men of being responsible for what they themselves criticize in women. More recent examples include the 20th-century poets Delmira Agustini, Alfonsina Storni, Juana de Ibarbourou, and Gabriela Mistral, winner of the Nobel Prize in 1945.

Taking as a point of departure the work of Sylvia Plath, Rosario Ferré, in her essay "Las bondades de la ira," makes an assessment of these Spanish-American poets' contribution to the development of female expression at the beginning of the century.[25] Ferré points out that while there are many similarities between Plath and the Spanish American poets—they struggled for the same ideals, their poems are always personal—there are also marked differences: "mientras las hispanoamericanas se hundieron a menudo en la amargura y en el resentimiento, entregándose, al sacrificio y a la autodestrucción; mientras que sus poemas, en la mayoría de los casos, no rebasan la queja y el lamento, los poemas de Sylvia son una afirmación de la fuerza de la mujer."[26] Cultural differences and the forty years that separate them are significant, Ferré suggests, because while Plath had the opportunity of becoming a professional writer whose poems can be considered political and radical, the Latin Americans were amateurs who did not dissociate themselves from mainstream values.

Moreover, in comparing Sylvia Plath and Erica Jong, Ferré attests to the changes that occurred between the 1950s and 1970s. To the ambivalence of the 1950s, when women wanted to be independent and at the same time enjoy the advantages of the "great American Dream," she opposes the feminism of the 1970s. These differences of emphasis were reflected, on the one hand, in an intellectual and abstract language and the pessimism of the 1950s, which resulted in madness and suicide as ways to escape reality, and on the other, in the optimism and the brutal—at times obscene—language of the 1970s, which used humor as a demystifying element. Ferré concludes that "en la obra de Erica, el cuadro de la mujer desconsolada, el cuadro de la mujer atrapada de los años '50 que nos representa Sylvia, ha sido afortunadamente superado."[27]

Taking an example from Mexican literature, we are able to observe some of these changes in the poetic itinerary of Rosario Castellanos, a poet who during her career radically reversed her position from anti-feminist to feminist. At the beginning of the sixties she changed her poetic style and abandoned symbolic and metaphoric language, thus breaking with the intellectual and abstract trends developed by other members of her generation in order to find her own voice.[28] Castellanos started to write an open and confessional poetry while ironically using myth and legendary figures. She not only read women authors from Latin America, Europe, and America, but she also wrote about them, revealing an increasing feminist awareness that grew more radical at the end of her life. In her poem "Meditación en el umbral," the speaker searches for new ways, new solutions for women.[29] Recalling Madame Bovary, Anna Karenina, Teresa de Avila, Sor Juana, Jane Austen, and Emily Dickinson, the poetic I rejects their methods, claiming that there has to be another way. Here Castellanos is using poetry as a vehicle to develop female consciousness.

The theme of self-discovery and self-identity in the works of women poets has been prominent in the English-speaking world since the 1920s, and it has intensified and acquired a stronger character in the last fifteen years.[30] Women poets have expressed their truth about their own lives by articulating sentiments and feelings that had been repressed or that had not been voiced before. Consequently there has been a deliberate and conscious process of finding a new literary language that is different from that of the patriarchy, many times free of metaphor, or at least using it in an innovative and subversive way. The use of colloquial, everyday language to examine what it means to be a woman and to discover the self—not only for one's own benefit but to help others by creating a consciousness of what this entails—has been the task of women poets in the past decades. For some such as Anne Sexton, who has spoken about intimate experiences and the domestic realm, poetry provides its creator with a social role, a mission, an activity that, according to Suzanne Juhasz, she:

> can send away to the world, a testimony of yourself. Words that will change the lives of those who read them and your own life too. So that you can know that you are not only the wife and mother, not only the rat, but that you are the poet, a person who matters, who has money and fame and prizes and students and admirers and a name.[31]

Testimonial poetry, confessional poetry, is not equivalent to natural language but is rather an artistic and literary language that has been cultivated by many female poets in recent years. In the American tradition, Sylvia Plath is famous for having created a confessional type of poetry characterized by openness. This openness differs from that which had been utilized earlier by male poets, for Plath discovers new poetic strategies to express openness from the female point of view.[32] In her poetic work, art and life are fused, or as Suzanne Juhasz has put it, "ultimately, we cannot distinguish between her situation, herself and her art."[33]

Despite the fact that in this type of referential poetry there is an obvious link between personal life and poetic creation, the reader must keep in mind that there is also a distance between the two marked by the process of artistic elaboration and selection. Since subjectivity has been transformed into an object, the poem becomes, as Sexton suggests, a vehicle for salvation, for it shows in a concrete fashion female activity and creativity.

An additional consideration that has been emphasized with respect to this kind of poetic expression is the fact that the relationship established between reader and speaker is non-hierarchical, thus allowing a non-elitist and more accessible communication with the reader. The attempt to close the gap between poet and reader so that the former can reach a larger audience through his or her art is not exclusive to women poets. In the Latin American tradition are the well-known cases of the Chilean poets Nicanor Parra, proponent of "antipoetry," and Pablo Neruda. With his *Odas elementales* Neruda initiated a new stage in his poetic development that was in accord with his political ideology and expressed his desire to communicate more easily with his readers.

Yet another function fulfilled by confessional poetry within the current feminist struggle has been its testimonial value. As Suzanne Juhasz has suggested, "writing poems from personal experience, feminine experience, is an act both necessary and vital for the revolution that is occurring. . . . We need before us the evidence in many forms of women and their lives. Feminist poets are giving us these lives."[34]

The poetic tendencies I have referred to in this essay are crucial to discussing Beverly Silva's poetry. When one examines the poems in this collection the presence of these two heritages becomes apparent: her work contributes to the exploration of the realities of yet another section of the female world, that of the Chicana.

In the confessional poems that constitute this collection the speaker not only identifies herself as female but describes both her physical and emotional condition as well:

> a woman in her forties
> my hair is colored
> my teeth are false
> maybe only my poems
> and my pain
> are real.
>
> ("Pounding down First St.")

21

Although in this poem the speaker refers to herself with first person pronouns, she uses the indefinite article when introducing her self-portrait, thus signaling that she is just "a" woman "in Copenhagen clogs" who, like many others, is about to start a new existence. Even though she colors her hair and has false teeth her life has not ended. The poetic I finds herself between two worlds, two stages of her life, between East and West, between motherhood and solitude, between the past and an uncertain future. She is searching for a purpose in a life that seems empty after her divorce and after her grown-up children have left. In addition, in spite of having earned an M.A. in English she has no job. But, just as she restores life to crumbled geraniums by "placing them in fresh water / in a salad dressing bottle," she has her own life restored by beginning to teach again as a volunteer. Her new activities and personal involvements allow her to feel again:

> from this ghost of a woman
> pounding First St.
> a form was emerging
> feeling coming from another language.

Here and in other poems her sense of fulfillment is determined by social relationships, by teaching, or by helping others as manager of the apartment complex where she lives.

At the end of this poem the speaker describes herself again, this time by enumerating her roles:

> & San José—
> wife, mother, student, woman alone,
> poet, teacher, lover,
> all i am and all i know
> is rooted in your streets.

Throughout this collection the speaker appears playing different roles in her female capacity: mother, neighbor, teacher, lover. In the poem "My Four Children" she assumes her role as mother when describing her children's physical and personality traits. Her offspring are all very different from each other and the speaker emphasizes this diversity. Each has left her to create an independent life away from her. In this poem the mother figure appears not as someone who would suffocate or try to control her children's lives but as one who sees and respects their differences and accepts their decisions. When her last daughter leaves home she feels empty and worthless but tries to accept her new reality of "woman alone."

In other poems the speaker shows her attachment to her neighborhood and its inhabitants, describing not only the people she sees in the streets but also the menial activities necessary for everyday survival:

> i love shopping at Tropicana Foods
> buying frijoles & southern greens & ten pound bags
> of Asian rice
> waiting in line with food stamps
> maybe having a drink at the Red Sparks before going home.
>
> ("East San José")

At the end of the poem the poetic I summarizes her pride in her barrio community, which she sees as an integral part of her own self:

> i love being here in the middle
> of this lowrider country
> sharing all the energy
> & feeling this pride
> in what i am.

The conflict of her different identities or roles is intensified by her Chicano background, and the theme of the divided self becomes apparent. In "Not because i love literature less," the speaker, torn between choosing life in the barrio close to her people and an intellectual dialogue at the university, decides to "seek a new knowledge" and immerse herself "in quiet / watching this new life around me." She emphasizes that in the barrio she is also learning new skills, though different from those she learned in school:

> i'm learning acceptance from my neighbors.
> i'm learning to live on beans and tortillas and beer without
> complaint.
> i'm learning about smiles and nods and non-verbal language
> i'd forgotten.

when i need conversation
there's a corner bar filled with characters as interesting
as any professor.
when i need love
there's a next door dance hall filled with romantic men
as handsome as my young dreams.

Through this type of life she is discovering real feelings and sentiments, "something i could never express to my intellectual friends / i forget now to call." While the university provides her with intellectual knowledge in a protected environment, life in the community is stormy. The new knowledge she is acquiring comes not from professors but from poverty, people, and feelings, which she cannot in turn convey to her former friends. The speaker is seeking what she thinks is lacking from her experience. In doing so she is searching for a bridge; she wants to have the two experiences but for the moment it does not seem feasible. Literature and university life to not seem to her to be real life, and she is determined to have a taste of the latter. Nevertheless, she cannot abandon forever her intellectual concerns, and in another poem, "Reading Lorna's Poems," she returns to the classroom, this time as a teacher. Her students, *alumnos,* make her task worthwhile and she is able to find through them the bridge between life and literature she was seeking for literature seems to be filled with life in reading Lorna's poems. Both life and literature are brought together, "knowing again that literature heals the hunger and the pain"; but even as she perceives that the two worlds cannot be separated, the intellectual question remains unanswered, for she cannot explain why it is so.

Of the 35 poems that make up this collection, about one third focus on the relationship between man and woman, an obviously important and central aspect of life for the speaker. I will now examine the type of relationships that are established between the speaker and her lovers.

In "José Luis" the poetic voice tells of the attraction that she, a "stranded intellectual," feels for this *macho* "intenso y serio" who speaks Spanish, wears Mexican-style clothes, sports a Villa moustache, and exhibits macho gestures—a proud man unable to read or write. However, even though she loves him she rejects him. Here we find the same conflict alluded to before in "Not because i love literature less"; the speaker is divided between her instinctive sexual attraction and her intellectual yearnings. Since this handsome man cannot offer her the unity she is seeking, she leaves him.

In "Mi negro amor malcontento" it is the speaker who is abandoned, but instead of suffering passively and submissively she actively looks for a new man. The poetic voice addresses her former lover saying, "i'm down on Second St. now seeking a new love." Emphasizing that it is not she who has lost him but he who has lost her, she adds "Ella que tú has perdido."

The way in which the poetic I describes and presents herself to the reader does not correspond to the image of the traditional woman who suffers in silence from her love wounds: on the contrary, just as men have always done, she has many suitors and lovers and establishes different types of relationships with them. Nevertheless, there is a certain ambivalence on the part of the poetic voice. In "He's Gone," for example, we are confronted with the speaker's contradictory feelings. Here her lover leaves at 3 a.m., thinking that she is asleep, but feeling empty and restless after he goes she cannot return to her bed. She tries to reclaim her lover's body by touching heself in order to catch "the imprint of his body / the frailty of bones shaking." Impotent and frustrated by the cool attitude of the mature and modern woman that she displayed when she saw him leaving, she decides that next time she will not keep quiet but will,

> scream
> plead
> hide his clothes
> before
>> he's gone

in the old-fashioned female style.

In the poem "Two Brothers," on the other hand, the speaker reverses the traditional situation in which the man views the woman as either wife and mother or prostitute. In this poem we are confronted with a female poetic voice who speaks of men as being like brothers who divide her life in two:

> One gives me kitchens
> & kids
> everyday phone calls

> punctuality
> fixes faucets & toilets
> brings me coffee in bed.
>> the other slips in late at night
> not speaking
> peels me like a banana
> loves until dawn
> leaves making no promises.

The speaker may be saying that she needs two men in order to be fulfilled as a woman, as men have asserted when they looked for pleasure outside the home, or she may be suggesting that woman, like man, has two sides in her love life—that of mother and wife and that of the senses—and that the man she loves should awaken both sides of her.

The speaker's love life is intense. She has loved and been loved passionately, but she has also suffered many wounds. In "i went to México, Mi Amor" she travels to Mexico to forget a lover who has gone back to his country and has not answered her letters. She has dreamt about this trip to Mexico and visits the places she has heard so much about: Puerto Vallarta, San Blas, Guadalajara, and so on. While fulfilling this ritual she finds a new love, a cab driver, and discovers Mexico. The poem is addressed to her former lover and ends with these ironic remarks:

> & Maybe someday, Mi Amor
> you'll meet my cab driver friend.
> But then i'm forgetting
> i went to México, Mi Amor
>
> to forget you.

The trip to Mexico is a ritual pilgrimage, a trip in search of her origins, but, nevertheless, a trip to a foreign world. When the speaker comes back to California she addresses her Mexican lover, saying that while she is "fiercely in love with your México," it is not hers.

The image of woman that emerges from these love poems is not that of the traditional Chicana attached to one man, her family, house and children, but a strong individual who participated in the student revolt of the late 1960s and the protests against United

States involvement in Vietnam—a modern woman, deeply rooted in her Mexican heritage but at the same time with a career and a life of her own.

Another aspect of Chicano culture Silva touches upon is the relationship between the Chicano and the white woman, the *gabacha*. Silva devotes two poems to the *gabacha* in which she exposes the double standard present in Chicano culture: Chicanos may have many women but they expect Chicanas to be faithful wives. In "Gabachas" we find two different speakers who represent two different points of view. On the one hand we have the *gabachas*, with whom Chicanos like to make love but whom they would never marry, and on the other, the Chicano:

> ¡Ay! To marry with a gabacha
> an hombre would have to be loco en la cabeza.
> The gabachas never have one man, but many.
> The mexicana lives for love and loves for life.
> Leave a gabacha for a few days or weeks, amigos,
> and otro hombre está en tus zapatos.

Just like Sor Juana in "Hombres necios," here Silva denounces men's double standard, emphasizing that they blame women for something that they themselves have caused.

There are still other poetic strategies used by the speaker that reflect Silva's Chicano background. For example, one significant, deliberate effect is the use of "i" in lower case for the poetic "I" even to start a sentence. Although this is not an original spelling, nor is it only used by Chicano poets—some other women poets also use it—it shows the speaker's stance, her position toward the world, the people, and the things she describes. It suggests that the poetic I considers herself an equal of those who surround her and that the emphasis is on communication, on sharing, and not on the self. In addition, other orthographic features suggest to the reader the intermingling of the two cultures. In the titles of the poems Silva uses both the English and the Spanish patterns of capitalization: one finds titles written with capitals and lower case (although the poet does not always capitalize all of the key words); titles with only an initial capital, as is done in Spanish; and titles that are all in lower case. The two all-Spanish titles also show this variation. The fact that there is no pattern that the reader can identify with one or the other language may appear arbitrary, but it also shows the degree of interaction between the poet's two linguistic codes.

Another feature that points toward the Chicano tradition is the emphasis on language and communication. In "Chaparral Super" the speaker and a friend eat Mexican food in a typically American locale, a supermarket parking lot:

> We sit in the parking lot with Tecate & carnitas
> salt, lemon & salsa between us.
> i can almost feel i'm in Mexico City
> staring at the mural
> with Raúl's voice going on & on
> in español that he thinks i understand
> every word of.
> both of us too drunk to care
> so i talk back in inglés
> as if he understood me.

Since they do not understand each other, communication is not accomplished at the level of articulated language but rather by sharing food and drinking Mexican beer, which is what they have in common, and, paradoxically, by looking at a mural they do not comprehend: "those giant faces / telling us god knows what." The poem suggests that although the speaker identifies with the Mexican tradition, it is not exactly her tradition because the absence of a common language prevents them from fully communicating.

Though we do find references to the protests of the late 1960s and early 1970s, such as in "San José State, 1978" and "letter to an old friend," it is clear from this last poem, where the speaker addresses a fellow student from the old days who continues to live in the past, that she is seeking to integrate and find her way in society. The mood is conciliatory and not disruptive. Even a forceful poem about wetbacks, which could have been used to protest their situation, has a rather subdued and matter-of-fact tone. The allusions to the Mexican revolutionary heroes Villa and Zapata function as "ethnic markers" to establish a cultural and historical linkage with the poet's Mexican roots, rather than serving as signs of subversion.[35]

In Silva's poetry we also notice the use of some devices that have been popular among other feminist writers, such as allusions to fairy tales or the use of traditional images in a subversive way. Using the legendary figure of the frog who is transformed into a prince, the speaker tells of how a persistent man, whom she had rejected because his appearance did not seem attractive to her, kept coming back. Ironically, just as in any number of love stories, his love won her over, and when she kissed him "a prince emerged" ("The Frog"). An example of the second strategy can be seen in her utilization of the image of the house with negative connotations. The house is no longer that protective and secure place where woman belongs, but instead a space that encloses her and shuts her off:

> Pain
>
> is a box.
> i'm in a box
> & i can't get out of it.
>
> It is a house.
> Walls and roof
> & a solid floor,
>
> but no door.

Silva's poetic persona emerges as a secure voice, distinctly feminine without being submissive or dependent. One does not find rebellious or angry overtones against machismo in these poems because the female poetic voice regards the male as an equal who—like her heritage, her children, her career, and her community—is an essential part of her life. These poems show that there is an alternative, even if a certain ambivalence remains. In "i'm going back some night" Silva proposes poetry and art as a means to resolve this conflict. The poetic I dreams of inscribing Raza poems on the walls of her old apartment complex and of giving it a new and more fitting name, *Little Chihuahua* instead of *Queen Anne*.

The Second St. Poems give testimony to a desire to integrate into society while stressing Chicano culture and values. Without forgetting her roots and from a basis of equality, the poetic I attempts to assert her individuality on a double level, sexual and cultural, and to integrate the personal and the social. By writing

MARIA INES LAGOS-POPE

primarily in English and by suggesting a movement toward integra-
tion into American society without forgetting the old traditions, and
by also adopting the attitudes and values of contemporary feminists, Silva is signaling the new direction of the Chicana. *The Second
St. Poems* show that Enriqueta Longanez' 1969 proposition is finally
becoming a reality, that there is hope to defeat machismo if women
are determined to fight for equality. The Chicana portrayed in these
poems is man's equal, an independent and self-supportive person
who belongs to an ethnic and cutural tradition and who needs
personal relationships with men, family, and community in order to
be content and fulfilled. From this point of view, by giving these
experiences a voice and by expressing the anxieties, interests, and
feelings of women in a changing world, Beverly Silva's work
constitutes a chronicle of personal and shared struggle.

STATE UNIVERSITY OF NEW YORK
AT BINGHAMTON

Notes

[1]The biographical information included here is based on a written statement provided by the poet.

[2]Margaret Atwood, in *Survival: A Thematic Guide to Canadian Literature* (Toronto: Anansi, 1972), has pointed out the similarities between women and Third World or other minority groups.

[3]José Armas, "Entrevista con Octavio Paz," *De Colores*, 2, No. 2 (1976), pp. 11-12.

[4]"The Space of Chicano Literature," *De Colores*, 1, No. 4 (1975), pp. 27-28.

[5]*Casa de las Américas*, 114 (1979), pp. 60-64.

[6]Ibid., pp. 63-4.

[7]"La poesía chicana: una nueva trayectoria," *The Identification and Analysis of Chicano Literature*, ed. Francisco Jiménez (New York: Bilingual Press/Editorial Bilingüe, 1979), p. 87.

[8]Felipe de Ortego y Gasca, "An Introduction to Chicano Poetry," *Modern Chicano Writers, A Collection of Critical Essays*, ed. Joseph Sommers and Tomás Ybarra-Frausto (Englewod Cliffs, NJ: Prentice Hall, 1979), p. 112.

[9]See Guadalupe Valdés-Fallis, "Code-Switching in Bilingual Chicano Poetry," *Hispania*, 59 (1976), p. 880.

[10]See Santiago Daydí-Tolson, "Voices from the Land of Reeds," forthcoming in his *Five Poets of Aztlán* (Ypsilanti, MI: Bilingual Press/Editorial Bilingüe, 1983), and Rolando Hinojosa, "Chicano Literature: An American Literature in Transition," *The Identification and Analysis of Chicano Literature*, pp. 37-40.

[11]Hinojosa, ibid., p. 38.

[12]"Literatura Chicana: Background and Present Status of a Bicultural Expression," *The Identification and Analysis of Chicano Literature*, p. 44.

[13]Interview with Juan Bruce-Novoa, *Latin American Literary Review*, 10 (1977), p. 112.

[14]"La poesía chicana: una nueva trayectoria," *The Identification and Analysis of Chicano Literature*, p. 85.

[15]"The Women of La Raza," *El Grito del Norte*, 2, No. 9 (July 6, 1969), reprinted in *Aztlán, An Anthology of Mexican-American Literature*, ed. Luis Valdez and Stan Steiner (New York: Knopf, 1972), p. 278.

[16]*Comparative Perspectives of Third World Women, The Impact of Race, Sex, and Class*, ed. Beverly Lindsay (New York: Praeger, 1980), pp. 246-47.

[17]"The Liberated Chicana, A Struggle Against Tradition," *Women, A Journal of Liberation*, 3-4 (1974), p. 42.

[18]"Hijas de Aztlán," *De Colores*, 1, No. 3 (1974), p. 42.

[19]See Gabriela Mora, "Narradoras hispanoamericanas: vieja y nueva problemática en renovadas elaboraciones," *Theory and Practice of Feminist Literary Criticism*, ed. Gabriela Mora and Karen S. Van Hooft (Ypsilanti, MI: Bilingual Press/Editorial Bilingüe, 1982), pp. 156-74.

[20]I discussed this topic in a paper entitled "Sumisión y rebeldía: el doble o la articulación literaria de la alienación femenina en cuentos de Marta Brunet y Rosario Ferré," read at the Conference on Latin American Women Writers held at Smith and Mount Holyoke Colleges on November 13, 1982.

[21]See Noemí Lorenzana, "Hijas de Aztlán," p. 40, and Maxine Baca Zinn, "Chicanas: Power and Control in the Domestic Sphere," *De Colores*, 2, No. 3 (1975), pp. 19-31.

[22]"La Mexicana, An Image of Strength," *Agenda*, Spring 1974, p. 4, quoted by Maxine Baca Zinn, "Chicanas: Power and Control in the Domestic Sphere," p. 25.

[23]See Noemí Lorenzana, "Hijas de Aztlán," p. 42.

[24]In the past decades Latin American women writers have devoted their efforts mainly to writing fiction.

[25]*Sitio a Eros* (México: Joaquín Mortiz, 1980), pp. 99-126.

[26]Ibid., p. 108.

[27]Ibid., p. 111.

[28]In "Si 'poesía no eres tú' entonces ¿qué?," *Mujer que sabe latín (México: SepsetentasDiana, No. 83, 1979)* Castellanos wrote: "*El pecado sin remisión de ambos poemas* ["Apuntes para una declaración de fe" y *Trayectoria del polvo*] es el vocabulario abstracto del que allí hice uso. Me era indispensable suplirlo por otro en el que se hiciera referencia a los objetos próximos, en el que los temas tomaran una consistencia que se pudiera palpar" (pp. 205-6). For a discussion of the open poetic style developed by Castellanos see Beth Miller, "Women and Feminism in the Works of Rosario Castellanos," *Feminist Criticism, Essays on Theory, Poetry and Prose*, ed. Cheryl L. Brown and Karen Olson (Metuchen, NJ: The Scarecrow Press, 1978), pp. 198-210.

[29]*Poesía no eres tú, Obra poética 1948-1971* (México: Fondo de Cultura Económica, 1972), p. 326. In her essay "María Luisa Bombal y los arquetipos femeninos," Castellanos elaborates on these same ideas when she states: "¿Basta vivir correctamente y morir correctamente? Desde luego que no. Pero como no existe ninguna otra alternativa real (¿vivir apasionadamente como Emma Bovary para terminar apurando un vaso de veneno? ¿Vivir desafiando los convencionalismos sociales como Anna Karenina para ser repudiada aún por su cómplice y suicidarse arrojándose al paso de un tren? ¿Vivir la aventura de Anita de Ozores y sembrar la desgracia en torno suyo y no soportar el peso de los remordimientos y desfallecer de locura a los pies de una divinidad implacable?) se inventan alternativas imaginarias," *Mujer que sabe latín*, pp. 147-8.

[30]See Judith Kegan Gardiner, "On Female Identity and Writing by Women," *Critical Inquiry*, 8, No. 2 (1981), p. 347.

[31]Suzanne Juhasz, "Seeking the Exit or the Home: Poetry and Salvation in the Career of Anne Sexton," *Shakespeare's Sisters, Feminist Essays on Women Poets*, ed. Sandra M. Gilbert and Susan Guber (Bloomington: Indiana University Press, 1979), p. 261.

[32]See Terence Diggory, "Armored Women, Naked Men: Dickinson, Whitman, and Their Successors," *Shakespeare's Sisters*, p. 145.

[33]" 'The Blood Jet': The Poetry of Sylvia Plath," *Feminist Criticism: Essays on Theory, Poetry and Prose*, p. 130.

[34]"The Feminist Poet: Alta and Adrienne Rich," *Feminist Criticism: Essays on Theory, Poetry and Prose*, p. 161.

[35]For the concept of "ethnic identity markers" see Guadalupe Valdés-Fallis, "Code-Switching in Bilingual Chicano Poetry," *Hispania*, 59 (December 1976), p. 882.

The
Second St. Poems

For my daughter Joy
who paid the rent

Second St.

           Second St.,
with a fierce passion i have claimed you.
With a fierce pride i have named a book of poems for you.
           As i stand here
balanced between East and West San José
weighing my life
you hold me.
           Like a well used shoe
no longer respectable or stylish
but comfortable as old leather
you hold me.
           Like a new lover
deftly withholding pleasure one moment
opening new dimensions of himself the next
you hold me.
           i walk the length of your pavement
writing poems.

The Cactus

November sunshine floods my kitchen window.
The plants thrive.
The lemon tree bursts with ripe fruit.
i measure the cactus.
Five inches of new growth
since that cold January afternoon
i found it.
Lone spindly thing like all the life here
on Second St.
uprooted and cast off in a corner of the alley
between Taconazo and my apartments.
i brought it home
laid wet paper towels on its roots
not knowing then
that almost nothing can kill a cactus.
i planted this dried up spike in a plastic pot
with dirt from the parking lot of this next door dance hall.
Taconazo dirt.

The cactus grows.
i eat nopalitos every morning with my breakfast.

Not because i love literature less

but because i love life more
i've left the University,
that refuge for a stormy life,
and i seek a new knowledge.
For days i speak only Spanish
or not at all.
i immerse myself in quiet
watching this new life around me.
Needing to know what i'd be
without an education.
Welfare and poverty are nothing new
accepting them is.
i'm learning acceptance from my neighbors.
i'm learning to live on beans and tortillas and beer without
                                                    complaint.
i'm learning about smiles and nods and non-verbal language
                                                    i'd forgotten.
when i need conversation
there's a corner bar filled with characters as interesting
as any professor.
when i need love
there's a next door dance hall filled with romantic men
as handsome as my young dreams.
They return me to a world of feelings
a belief in love and sentiments
something i could never express to my intellectual friends
i now forget to call.
Not because i love literature less
but because i love life more
i'm content to sit here at this window
waiting for the next chapter.

The roaches came from everywhere

under
over
above
behind
between
around
below
it was a lesson in prepositions to ponder them.
Big ones
small ones
medium sized ones
families & communities of them invaded our apartment.

My method was attack.
with spray can & poison i'd hit & run.
Joy preferred to crush them
with an old butter knife she kept ready for this purpose.
She was slow & meticulous about crunching each one.

At night they crawled from all the cracks
to cover our walls like some grotesque canvas
painted by a madman.

To move wasn't possible,
we had to fight.

Joy bought caulking compound
& puttied all the corners of all the cupboards.

They rose from the linoleum.

An extermination bomb was our only hope.
but we'd have to vacate for three days
& where could we go?
They always return anyway, we were told.
Through the walls from the neighbors.

People move out
others move in
& the roaches are back.

So we resigned ourselves
to sharing our living quarters with them.
Joy continued crunching with her butter knife.
i lapsed into quiet
with only occasional outbursts of spray can mania.

The roaches became my nemesis.
Sharing these vermin bound me forever to my neighbors.
The temporariness of our situations became enhanced
by rejections of our mutual suffering,
pretense of waiting lists for better apartments,
or savings for deposit money.
Easier to live with roaches when:

We're going to move from here any time now.

Chaparral Super

We sit in the parking lot with Tecate & carnitas
salt, lemon & salsa between us.
i can almost feel i'm in Mexico City
staring at the mural
with Raúl's voice going on & on
in español that he thinks i understand
every word of.
both of us too drunk to care
so i talk back in inglés
as if he understood me.
   we eat carnitas
   share the salsa
   stare at the mural
   those giant faces
   telling us god knows what
¡Viva México!
salud & all that
we toast with a 6-pack of Tecate
in a supermarket parking lot
on a Saturday afternoon.

Pounding down First St.

alone
on a Mother's Day Sunday
packing for storage
the invitation from Arizona
safe in my bag
phone calls for companionship
and assistance on this day
bringing me nothing.
but—"you can stay with me
a couple of weeks
before you leave"
said Joy,
my youngest child.

> this 18 year old daughter
> 6 months on her own
> in a 2 room apartment
> where i helped kill roaches
> the day we moved
> from one home
> to 2 separate ones.

i came to Second St.
the day after Mother's Day
all my belongings in Bekins
for a short visit to my daughter
before leaving for Arizona.

i came with 3 suitcases
a wicker basket filled with books
and a canvas bag packed with poems,
literary awards, a not yet one year old
Master's Degree,
and a one way ticket from California
home of my birth.

> friends of 13 years
> letters from South America
> England and Europe
> children the age of mine

                    in Arizona now
                    sending long distance replies
                    to my cries for help.
only a couple of weeks.
ghost of a woman
wandering First St.
wondering on this liberated daughter
separated from me
nearly 5 of her teenage years
now sharing her two rooms
with a boyfriend
and me silent
as the ancient Chinese.
                    a woman in her forties
                    my hair is colored
                    my teeth are false
                    maybe only my poems
                    and my pain
                    are real.
pounding down First St.
in Copenhagen clogs
symbol of my short career
as part-time
temporary leave replacement
College English Instructor.
& now each step beating out
this unresolved hunger
like the unused Master's Degree
so bright and new
& for what?
for what?
for what?

clenching the Arizona ticket
avoiding a departure
clinging to this native land
with the same fierceness
that carried me
to a college degree.

                    & for what?
                    i haven't seen San Francisco
                    in two years
                    it's been five
                    since i lay on the beach
                    at Santa Cruz
                    the sights of San José
                    lie between the University
                    and the welfare office
                    my poems are unpublished
                    my resumé unread
                    & Mother's Day
                    stale as last year's
                    Whitman's samplers.
First St.
incredible dividing line
betweend East and West
the Los Gatos hills of my youth
green as that young girl running off
to be married.
the East foothills
bare as those struggling years
as student and mother
divorced and alone.

pounding down First St.
in wooden clogs
grasping crumbled geraniums
from the car wash
as if they were direct transplants
from Neruda's Chile
his bitter and thirsty flowers
crying out for existence.
placing them in fresh water
in a salad dressing bottle
blazing emblem in this apartment window
of my search and demand
O yes Neruda—¡yo también
pido silencio y amor sin fin!

poems and books
on a kitchen table
crowded with unwashed dishes
flour and dried up beans on my typewriter
the stale smell of empty cans of Coors
a butterknife Joy uses to kill roaches
half nights of sleeping in a bed
before Joy and Gabe return
from pool and pitchers of beer
tortillas at midnight
all of us crazy and drunk
i shake flour from my papers
save my books from lard
curl into the wornout sofa
to finish a night's sleep
with only beer to numb this pain.

        Gabe asks me to teach him English
        confides in me how little he knows
        i find the school
        hide this Master's Degree
        like an albatross
        overqualifying me
        work as a volunteer
        conceal this activity
        from the Welfare Dept.

3 hours a day
with the beautiful teacher
with her beautiful daughter
little angel girl sitting in class
day after day
weaving patterns
into the fabric of my life.

        What are you doing?
        Are you learning English?
        Are you happy?
        Are you sad?
        Oh, I'm sorry.

        Dear Chela,
        do you know you allowed me to feel
                       again?

44

from this ghost of a woman
pounding First St.
a form was emerging
feeling coming from another language.

Estoy aprendiendo.
Estoy feliz.
Estoy trabajando.
Y yo soy una maestra.
i return the Arizona ticket
buy a bicycle
make a path to and from the school
the tracks daily deepening
pulling me ever tighter into this soil
where i was born.
& San José—
wife, mother, student, woman alone,
poet, teacher, lover,
all i am and all i know
is rooted in your streets.

José Luis

Certainly not worth a poem
only a photograph between the pages of my journal.
"Who does he think he is?"
my daughter asked when he had the photo taken
and presented it to me.
But i smiled.
It takes macho to do that.

José Luis.
The blue silk shirt from Mexico
extravagantly emphasized by white trousers
legs spread
left foot on the bar rail
right hand on his hip
a Coors carefully cupped in the left
elegant in shoulder length black hair
heavy Villa moustache.
All so intenso y serio.

José Luis.
Maybe you are worth a poem.
Un canto para hombre macho
from me
this feminine bard
stranded on Second St.
writing odes to dark eyed men
in exchange for a new language.
"Estoy aprendiendo,"
i say now before my lips are closed with kisses
my hair fluffed loose
by tender hands.

José Luis.
Don't you know i'm only playing?
enthralled by the intricacies of your enunciation
feeling like those early anthropologists

recording new languages known only by sound.
Stranded intellectual
never having met a man unable to read or write.

José Luis.
Thoughtfully i place your photo in my journal.
Mi hombre macho.
Mi amigo tan intenso y serio.
"Sí, te quiero mucho,"
——now leave!
You really aren't worth a poem.

Mi negro amor malcontento

i'll write no more poems for you
my sulky black love.
My tears won't fall again
into a legal sized envelope
mailed to you.
i'm down on Second St. now seeking a new love.
A brown skinned man this time
with curly hair
skin tight pants
& platform shoes.
Un hombre macho he'll be
loving me on the dance floor
with a red bandana
to tie our wounds.
Nieto de Villa y Zapata.
¡Bandidos gloriosos!
¡Los intrépidos!
Not like you
tall one from the islands
always seeking your shadow
chasing love from your door.
¡Extranjero!
Some night you will awaken
to a sweat drenched bed
clutching your pillow
calling my name.
& Me?
Ella que tú has perdido.
¿Dónde estará?
Down on Second St.
dancing with a brown skinned man
with a red bandana.
¡Mi negro amor malcontento!

He's Gone

Awake to the cold chill
of his leaving at three a.m.
one eye watching him dress
levis firmly zippered
boots one by one
a shrug into the white T-shirt
thinking i'm asleep
he's gone.
sleep goes with him.
shuddering
i slip into a chenille robe
pulling the belt tight.
he's gone.
hands slide to a throbbing pelvis
seeking the imprint of his body
the frailty of bones shaking
against this chill.
he's gone.
tires cry outside my window
leaves whisper it.
he's gone. he's gone.
Second St. lies before me in early dusk
always a near siren
flashing red lights that penetrate my bedroom drapes
speeding traffic
the eternal freeway overhead
insomniac neighbor who paces
coughs
flushes the toilet
plays soft music
shares these early morning hours with me
but
he's gone.
at five a.m. i close the drapes
return to bed
to sheets cold as an untouched meal
to tears against will and reason.
he's gone.

next time
i'll cry first
scream
plead
hide his clothes
before
        he's gone.

Depression

is like a door closing.
Arms tied behind me
unable to struggle.
A gag in my mouth
unable to scream.
Tears flood my eyes
there is no reason.
Rage beats at my senses
my body is numb.
No one calls
i've always been the outgoing one.
i crawl within myself
staring out this window
day after day
waiting to die.

General Assistance is as low as you can get

Like you've got nothing
& you're eligible for nothing.
Not sick enough for disability
never worked enough for unemployment
not blind
or 65
or crazy
or hooked on drugs or drink
can't claim Aid to Families with Dependent Children
'cause you got no kids living with you
& you own nothing.
No real estate boats campers trailers
jewelry stocks & bonds life insurance.
Your car—if you got one—is over five years old
& your furniture totals less than $5000.
You sign papers testifying to this fact
before the personal interview.
The social worker i met said she never learned in school
about this aid & wasn't i fortunate it's available.
Of course, she added, unlike other aid
this must be paid back.
Papers must be signed giving the county a claim
to future real estate holdings.
Those are county funds, you see,
so it's not like a state or federal grant.

Real estate was far from my mind
the day i walked from that welfare office
my eligibility affirmed
my total worth consisting of crates of books
& a heart filled with dreams.
i returned to my $60 a month room
looked at my $109 monthly grant
& said General Assistance really is as low as you can get.
Someday i'll write a poem about that.

Always close to death on Second St.

there's no way to escape knowledge of mortality
living on Second St.
with only a pane of glass separating you from the prostitutes,
dance hall music entering all your windows,
& a mortuary across the street.
Downtown violence is a thing you live with:
all night sirens,
barroom knifings,
once a month eruptions from people on dope or booze
wrecking their apartments.
Poverty and frustration speak out.
Every few months there's a murder,
an unidentified body
the police always link to dope or passion or prostitution.
& Nearly every day there's a funeral,
cars lined up for blocks following the black hearse.
Who could ever forget their mortality
living this close to death?
Still, who is prepared for the stranger
who breaks in late at night
leather jacket and fist in the face
all that can be remembered.
Scared away by a chance visitor
no one knows if his motive was rape, burglary, or murder.
The cars pass your window the next day
following the black hearse.
Home from emergency hospital,
always close to death on Second St.

The Frog

(For Ray Cisneroz)

You were my frog
a horny toad
hopping into my life.
i tried to send you on your way
like the others
but you kept coming back.
Every Friday i'd be cleaning
when you'd drop by
just to tell me how pretty i was.
            "Was i disappointed in you?"
you asked when we first met
after those weeks of phone calls.
Of course i was, but i said no.
You certainly weren't six feet tall
your sheepskin vest couldn't hide the beginning of a beer belly
your popeyes were bloodshot and stared at me nervously
& your puffy cheeks and upper lip had a sulkiness
i distrusted.
            But you kept coming back
every Friday. & Then
you had me laughing
when you bounced off my walls
so drunk that night.
            You were nicer than the hot bath
i was running when you came again.
Warmer than a puppy.
More playful than a remembered dog
i loved so fiercely when a young girl.
& All the other memories of love and possessiveness
locked away in silent corners of my soul
you were pulling from me week after week.
            Wasn't it by then inevitable
that when i kissed you
a prince emerged?

Two Brothers

One gives me kitchens
& kids
everyday phone calls
punctuality
fixes faucets & toilets
brings me coffee in bed.
              the other slips in late at night
not speaking
peels me like a banana
loves until dawn
leaves making no promises.

Debby

Debby is a Russian novel.
She is Dolohov balanced in a window sill high above Petersburg
chug-a-lugging a bottle of rum.
She speaks English, Spanish and Russian indiscriminately,
writes poetry on bathroom walls,
seduces her students.

She is the most corrupt woman i've ever known.
Overcome by the mass on Easter Sunday,
she hungers for the body of Christ,
tempts me to take communion,
without confession,
or baptism.

She is an enigma.
A Polish, Mexican, Midwesterner
rolling into California
to unsettle our easy ways,
like a new Rock song,
discordant and abrasive,
but impossible to ignore.

My Four Children

Joy is a brown girl.
Golden and brown
with the Azores sun sparkling through her.
High school drop-out,
she wheels through San José with a fake I.D.
to pool halls and beer busts,
her pizza parlor wages supporting us
all that year i finished college.

Madelyn is dark and delicate.
Mysteries of the Moors
whisper through her.
Shy as a sparrow
with black romantic eyes,
holding her husband and baby when barely 17.

Carla is yellow and frail.
The mark of the leprechauns
was left by her Irish father.
She reads the Bible to avoid anger,
covers her head with a scarf,
seeks Jesus for her lover.
Un-wed mother,
waiting for her baby to be returned.
Little black grandson i've never seen.

Jeff is a circle,
a smell of incense,
a Hare-Krishna chant,
a dream i've forgotten.
Address Unknown:
he's light years away from me,
black and red and silver neon,
psychedelic as the 1960's.

Wetbacks

used to cross the river
& sometimes their backs got wet.
They wanted to enter the promised land
make a few dollars at minimum wage or less
then split back to their families.
Nada más
y no problemas.
    Only there's a fence
between Baja and California, U.S.A.
climb the fence
drop down to the highway below
& run for the woods.
    Only it's not done that way.
You need a good coyote to bring you across
know when the guard changes
give you a bed for the night
a plate of frijoles before departure
cross the check point with papers intact
& deliver you up to L.A.
$300 for services rendered.
Then you can make a few American dollars
split back to the family
y no problemas.
    Only the family writes,
los niños necesitan ropa
el papá está enfermo
no hay mucha comida
& if otro hermano could make American dollars
to send home...
    Only it takes much saving for the coyote
to bring the brother across.
Then waiting in an L.A. cantina
an empty car arrives,
the brother's in a Tijuana jail
& the coyote's very sorry
but a no good hombre,
immigration man,
give him the doublecross.

¡Y chingada!
You know how these things are.
¡Así es la vida!
   The family writes again,
the brother is sick,
many bruises from los policías.
Necesita un mejor coyote.
& It takes much money
for a better coyote.
   Eighteen year old wetback
only looking for a job
washing dishes for American dollars.
Nada más
y no problemas.

Staying high with Debby

after Proposition 13
that California malady
that took away our jobs.
My career struck down before it barely started.
She's lucky to have a man's credit cards
a man she's waiting to leave.
All i have is my expertise on downtown living.
So we're staying high
touring First St. bars
eating at uptown restaurants.
Two years out of grad school
i'm still only a step away from the welfare office.
Teachers no longer needed.
Education struck down in California.
We sit in First St. bars drinking pitchers of beer
reminiscing about our respective years in the Universities.
Staying high with Debby
when there's nothing else to do.

San José State, 1978

Old revolutionary
sacked out on a bench in the Student Union
10 years gone
since Seventh St. blazed with speeches;
after too many jailings
a wife gone gay
Timothy Leary proved insane,
you sleep.

Fraternities gather outside
rallying the football season
Happy Hour on campus in the old cafeteria
the new bookstore throbbing with well dressed students
buying initialed T-shirts and graduation rings
on Visa cards.
The revolution is resigned to books on a dusty shelf
a low enrollment Sociology course
not included in next year's curriculum.

Old revolutionary
are you dreaming of Dow Chemical?
Vietnam Protests?
The Black Panther Party?
Free Speech and Human Rights?
The National Guard called to campus?

Old S.D.S. leader
i remember you—
we had coffee together
your eyes intense and steady
when you gave me reasons to boycott classes.
i was a housewife then
turned part time student and revolutionary
brave as i'll ever be
—i think.

i remember you
heard all your story
watched you wander the campus
vacant eyed
these past years.
when you came too close
i walked the other way
to avoid your sadness.

letter to an old friend

Dear John,
i hate to tell you this
John,
but
the hippies are dead
& if you want to get a girl
John,
you got to make some changes.
Like,
please forgive me
John,
but you got B.O.
when you don't smell of stale marijuana
& your beard hasn't been cleaned
since the late 60's.
Now i haven't turned establishment
John,
but like i said
the hippies are dead
& your Goodwill clothes & love beads
just don't make it now.
Sure, i miss you, John,
but
the cockroaches in your pad
aren't funny anymore
a girl gets tired of sharing the sofa
with your dog
& somehow two master's degrees
don't make up for a night on the town.
i still remember the good times we used to have
drinking Red Mountain in the park
& the free Wednesday night movies
but John,
please understand & forgive me
when i tell you
i met this guy with a Trans Am.

& He was all decked out in silk & turquoise
& i can't really explain it
but John,
times have changed.
If you want to get a girl now
get with it.

i dream of mexican murals and a community affair

it's not an easy place to live
on Second St.
i moved into the manager's apartment
after a knifing.
i moved out of that apartment
the complex, & all of Second St.
after an assault
& rental dispute hearings.
the two and a half years between these events
i dreamed of mexican murals & a community affair.

but not at first.
those first days of nothingness & pain
were spent at an open window
watching over an incredible under the freeway parking lot
owned by a nextdoor dance hall
but used by everyone.
people passing through town slept in their cars
truckers parked for a few days
police had their check points here
lovers met on lunch hours or after work
others came just to drink beer
prostitutes made their connections
old & young men stopped to piss beside the concrete posts
as if no one could see them
the mexican guys from the apartments worked on their cars
usually all day Saturdays
leaving littered beer cans for the Sunday morning recycle collector
page after page of my journal
became filled with these events.
i dreaded evening when i had to shut the drapes.

the manager's apartment was different.
larger & softer with windows on three sides
& a lemon tree that hovered protectively over my kitchen,
a forever part of my dreams.
thirteen mailboxes were lined side by side
a step from my kitchen window

where i watched tenants pause to sort through letters
glance at flyers from funeral homes & politicians
or read magazines belonging to someone else.
once a month they began knocking on my door
to pay the rent.
little by little i was forced out
of a painful shyness.
little by little i took over
the management of downtown apartments.
i don't know when i began to dream
of mexican murals & a community affair
but always there was this precarious balance
of loyalty to an owner
& natural sympathies with the tenants.

for my $60 a month rent reduction
i pushed brooms & pulled hoses
over a garbage littered cement expanse in front of the apartments
a back alley carport
& the side area of Second St.
sometimes the guys came out to help.
we'd drink beer & talk of barbecues & apartment parties
that only happened one time as a going away celebration
for Daniel who returned to his home in Chihuahua.

always i cleaned the laundry last.
always i planned to buy paint & brighten the dirty walls.
little by little my images spread out of the laundry
onto the large flat empty walls facing the freeway & parking lot.
colors became shapes in my mind
& my mexican murals were formed.

"you'd do the same as me if you were in my place,"
the owners always said. & how many times
in over forty years of life have i heard this?
i still argue & i still dream of community affairs.
housing for people & not for profit.
Second St. blazing with pride.
murals so startling that even the freeway
will stop to look.

i sleep quiet now.
no emergencies at my door.
no sirens that last all night.
dead bolt & safety locked windows
& a complex with twenty-four hour security guards.
for the first time in three years
i've remembered what heat is
& what plumbing is supposed to do.

only at midnight i awaken to these dreams of mexican murals
& a community affair. & i cry out:
                    can this much of me be claimed
                    yet i walk away with nothing?

Two Men in Chihuahua

two wounds inside me now.
strange that i should love another
who slipped behind that Tortilla Curtain
into Chihuahua.
two letters now
sit in postoffices
no reclamadas.

One at La Frontera
waits for my Juárez lover
who came to me so many nights
only after the bars had closed
knocking at my window
until i awakened.
he went to Juárez
for a family visit
for only a month
to Juárez where the bars
never close. & he
never returned.

The other waits
in San Francisco Del Oro
for an intense dark man
descended from a long line
of silver miners.
confused & scared
by American ways
guilt ridden from things he'd done
he returned to his mother
for comforting.

My letters sit
no reclamadas.
Only Chihuahua
has claimed these men.

Reading Lorna's Poems

Two hours between classes
& i'm the teacher now
why is it i still understand
only poems of hunger and rebellion?
Two hours between classes
it's raining now and turning dark
i drink wine, read on and forget
the lesson plans i've been trained to always remember.
Two hours between classes
knowing they'll understand. Mis alumnos.
The only ones really that matter. The ones
i do it all for.
Two hours between classes
Lorna. Lorna. You make it all real
again. You tell me what i am.
& Why i'm still doing what i am.
Two hours between classes
i've heard you read many of these poems.
Why are they so different, more vital and real printed up
& published in a pretty book?
Two hours between classes
reading Lorna's poems
knowing again that literature heals the hunger and the pain.
But i still don't know why.

Pain

is a box.
i'm in a box
& i can't get out of it.

It is a house.
Walls and a roof
& a solid floor,

but no door.

Two Finger Bob

After Vietnam he didn't give a shit.
came back better than some
only parts of his kidneys
three fingers
& a testicle
left behind.
sterile, but able to perform normally.
would've killed himself
if he'd lost that.

Back in the U.S. he rode a bike to California
kicked back in a commune
before joining the Angels.
they gave him the name, Two Finger Bob.
his biker's patch showed two fingers upright
along with the name.
it sits in a cigar box with clippings of his trial
pictures of his ex-wife
& the medal of honor.
he served four years in prison for dealing
passed the time with body building.

He works off & on in construction now
supplements it with disability
gets high on weekends
a little pot laced with hash
sleeps on a waterbed
& watches porny movies from Sweden.

He still doesn't give a shit.

only a dance hall pickup

what did i expect
when i loved a campesino?
that he'd treat me like a queen
or a virgin in a white gown
or even like a friend?

i was only a dance hall pickup
the night our worlds became one

weekends we spent together
long hours talking
telling me stories
about the women who work in the fields
how they like nice things
demand men with good cars
who take them to restaurants and dancing
on Saturday nights.
he had no girlfriend, he told me
because he had no money, no job right then.

but you have me
i'd contradict.
ah, but you're better than that
he'd explain.

yet i was only a dance hall pickup
the night our worlds became one

weekends i'm alone now
only long telephone calls where we fight
and he asks me not to go dancing
although he can't be with me
& gives no reason.

what did i expect
when i was only a dance hall pickup
the night our worlds became one.

Hey You!

Love comes heavy
lays me low
sends me running all over town
seeking your moustache
black eyes that penetrate
but aren't yours
so i turn
finding arms not yours
too weak for holding
late at night
calling
"come back,
come back"
we weren't made for sad endings
you & i.

Sin Ti Yo No Soy Nada

Tú eres
La salsa en mi enchilada
La carne en mi burrito
La oliva en mi tamal
El chocolate en mi mole
El chile en mis frijoles
La tequila en mi margarita.
       Seguramente yo puedo vivir sin ti, mi amor;
Pero sin ti la vida es
Un taco sin tortilla
El guacamole sin aguacate
La sal sin limón
Un pastel sin azúcar
El domingo sin baile
La cumbia sin música
Juan Gabriel sin Juárez
       Y todos los días sin el fin de semana.

i went to México, Mi Amor

to forget you.
i wanted to see Pancho Villa's house
the Noa-Noa club in Juárez
the silver mines so much a part of you
& ride the Chihuahua railroad.
But you didn't answer my telegram
so i went to México, Mi Amor

to forget you.
i flew over Sonora, Sinaloa & Nayarit
never touched Chihuahua
with my plane following the coastline
landing in far away Jalisco
at the Bay of Flags.
Three days in the exciting port of Vallarta
i only thought of you once
when i mailed you the postcard of the Caballito Del Mar
& also sent you a Happy Birthday greeting.

When your birthday came, Mi Amor
i was checking into a hotel
in San Blas, Nayarit.
i sent you a card from there
with another Happy Birthday greeting.
Wanted you to know i was traveling
over the mountains
and through the jungle
visiting México all by myself

to forget you.
Ten days later i pulled into Guadalajara
on a Las Estrellas Blancas camión
thinking how surprised you'd be
to know a dream of mine had come true.
i wanted to send you a giant size postcard
but i ran out of pesos
& had a few problems getting back home.

A cab driver came to my rescue,
Carlos Pérez Castañeda,
& he's my friend for life now.
Someday i'll tell you everything that happened
how i finally got on a plane
that flew all the way straight to Los Angeles
& i was running home scared and broke
but deliriously happy
fiercely in love with your México.

& Maybe someday, Mi Amor
you'll meet my cab driver friend.
But then i'm forgetting
i went to México, Mi Amor

to forget you.

Nopalito

was a skinny kid from Zacatecas.
weekends he sat in the clubs
drinking 7-Up with only a twist of lime
looking for a girlfriend.

at age 27
he claimed to be a reformed alcoholic
told me he used to get drunk every day
when he was just a child in Mexico
because there was nothing else to do.

so he got in trouble with the law eventually
and if he went home now
would have to go to prison.

my poet's mind made him an exile
& the next logical step
was a political refugee.

why he reminded me of the cactus in my kitchen window
was another logical step
for a skinny kid from Zacatecas
where all the cacti grow.

if he could have spoken English
he would have laughed at our jokes
he would have known we saw him as something romantic.
his exile, his name.

but he didn't.
he went back to the clubs
where he sits sipping 7-Up
looking for a girlfriend.

Gabachas

they call us.
Oh les gustan us mucho
our blue eyes and white skin.
También, they like very much
to have amor with us,
but nunca,
nunca, nunca,
would they marry us.
¡Ay! To marry with a gabacha
an hombre would have to be loco en la cabeza.
The gabachas never have one man, but many.
The mexicana lives for love and loves for life.
Leave a gabacha for a few days or weeks, amigos,
and otro hombre está en tus zapatos.

¡Chingada!
What can we do?
the hombres plead.
The gabachas like to fuck with us.
Chango que a la changa chinga.
Y sabemos que nada más they want us for.
¡Qué lástima!
They are so pretty.

Mamacita of the Burrito Wagon

doesn't like gabachas.
her sons don't like them either.
she asks them what they think of the gabachas who like it hot.
she speaks in front of the gabachas
because they no saben.
she watches them go in & out of the dances.
not many stop to buy a burrito.

Mamacita plumps pieces of meat in her mouth
as she slaps the tortillas.
she weighs maybe three hundred and fifty pounds.
she has a son at each elbow.
they assure her of how ridiculous the gabachas look to them.
"Todas están flacas & enfermas,"
the son on her right declares
his back turned to us.

Debby's chin drops & she blinks at me.
i puff out my overweight gabacha self
& smile at the son on her left.
he winks at us.
we pay mamacita & say goodbye in polite english.

she still has the best burritos in town.

East San José

i love cruising down King Road
on a Sunday afternoon
watching all those shiny lowriders
hydraulics bouncing when they stop
for red lights.

i love living in East San Jo
watching all the changes
like old Story Road
being called The Boulevard now.

i love swinging the King & Story corner every afternoon
cutting through the barrio to my apartment
looking at the distinctly California ranch style houses
built in the mid-fifties
& predicted to fall apart in twenty years.

i love shopping at Tropicana Foods
buying frijoles & southern greens & ten pound bags
of Asian rice
waiting in line with food stamps
maybe having a drink at the Red Sparks before going home.

i love looking at the cholos and cholas
guys with pompadours like old time movie stars
girls with painted cheeks
like circus clowns.

i love being here in the middle
of this lowrider country
sharing all the energy
& feeling this pride
in what i am.

Weekends Alone

Sometimes you got nothing else
& you have to
close & lock the door
knowing your rent is paid.

i'm going back some night

to those Second St. apartments i gave so much of my life to
& walked away with only a book of poems
& a sweet lover.
i'm going back with a spray can of red paint
a ladder
& a large neon sign,
a sign proclaiming the rightful name of these apartments.
Not *Queen Anne,* an impossible 1940's leftover,
but *Little Chihuahua*
for Daniel, Pedro, Víctor, Alfredo, Héctor, Ricardo, Sweet Lauro
& all the other guys from San Francisco del Oro
who paid their rent faithfully for 3 years
never complaining about increases
or lack of repairs.
i'm going to place that neon sign
with *Little Chihuahua* in red & yellow & blue lights
on the roof at eye level with the freeway
where all the cars going by on 280
will have to acknowledge it.
& then i'm going to take my spray can of red paint
& blast La Raza poems over every inch
of stucco and concrete.
When the sun rises
i'll head for my new home in lowrider land
safely away from downtown violence
able to sleep now without troubled dreams.

Previous Publications by Beverly Silva

"Poet." In *Reed.* San José, CA: San José State University, 1975, p. 26.

"This Is No Poem: This Is A Woman." *Women Talking, Women Listening* (Dublin, CA), Vol. III (Nov. 1977), pp. 6-7.

"Tears." *Women Talking, Women Listening,* Vol. IV (Nov. 1978), p. 39.

"Of Mice & Men." *The Sow's Ear* (Pittsburg, CA: The Blue Collar Press), Vol. II, No. 1.

"Afternoon Class," "Tan Triste," and "Commiserations upon losing." *Caracol* (San Antonio, TX), Vol. 5, No. 3 (Nov. 1978), pp. 7, 19, 20.

"Ms. Dickinson" and "To My Cunt." *Albatross* (East Orange, NJ), Summer 1978, pp. 36, 38.

"The forgotten student." *Mati 7* (Chicago, IL: Omnation Press), Spring-Summer 1978, p. 16.

"The Man I Love." *Mango* (San José, CA), Vol. I, Nos. 3 & 4 (Spring 1978), p. 16.

"Graduation Night, Part II." *Women Talking, Women Listening,* Vol. V (Nov. 1979), p. 2.

"Just kicking back with a 6-Pak." *Mango,* Vol. II (Winter 1979-80), p. 61.

"i have no poem this week." *Womankind* (Indianapolis, IN), Vol. II, No. xiv (1980), p. 9.

"Mother & Wife." *Off Our Backs* (Washington, DC), Vol. X, No. 10 (Nov. 1980), p. 15.

"Second St.," "Memories of a San José Winter," and "Beautiful Bikers." *California in Rhyme and Rhythm, I* (Hayward, CA: California Historical Society), May 1980, pp. 68, 75, 76. "Second St." rpt. in this volume.

"Untitled," "You see," and "Abstract." *The Poet* (Mishawake, IN), Autumn 1980, pp. 109, 286, 334.

"Nunca Más." *New Voices* (Methuen, MA), No. 1 (Fall 1980), p. 33.

"The Real World" and "The Green Witch." *Wellspring* (Monsey, NY), Vol. I, No. 2 (1980), pp. 8, 9.

"To a Stepfather" and "i have locked my M.A. degree in a safety deposit box." *Crazy Ladies* (Jan Glading, ed., Berkeley, CA), February 1981, pp. 41, 42, 43.

"Easter Sunday." *Visions #6.* Wheaton, MD: Black Buzzard Press, 1981.

"Hey You!" *Broken Streets* (Bristol, CT), Vol. III (1981), p. 9. Rpt. in this volume.

"To a Male Critic." *Snippets* (University Heights, OH: Pin Prick Press), Vol. II, Nos. 9 & 10 (Sept.-Oct. 1981).

"Arithmetic." *Snippets,* Vol. III, Nos. 1 & 2 (Jan.-Feb. 1982).

"You'll do to ride the river with." *Songs—A Singing of Poems by Unordinary Poets.* Murray, KY: 1982, p. 32.

Beverly Silva, born in Los Angeles, currently lives in San José, Californi Wanting to be a creative writer sinc her teenage years and secretly writir stories that she had to hide from he family, she was frustrated in her educational goals by being placed in vocational-secretarial course of studies. Three marriages and four children ensued. Finally attending college in the late 1960s, Silva, who was by this time struggling for survival as a single parent, was able to graduate with an M.A. in English from San José State University in 1976. She is currently a teacher of English as a Second Language in Adult Education.

Silva's poetry has been published in *Women Talking, Women Listening; Caracol; Albatross; Mango; California in Rhyme and Rhythm, I; The Poet; Womankind; Crazy Ladies; Broken Streets* and *Snippets. The Second St. Poems* is her first collection to be publishe as a book.

Bilingual Press/Editorial Bilingüe